Carols for Schools
Edited by John Rutter

Twelve carols for unison voices (with some optional parts), recorders or flutes, tuned percussion, untuned percussion, guitar, and piano.

Preface

Carols for Schools has been compiled to meet the needs of teachers looking for carols in which young singers and instrumentalists can both participate. The twelve carols selected (most of which have been specially arranged or adapted for this collection) are intended for unison singing, some with optional second voices, descants or rounds, and they feature a variety of instrumental accompaniments. Instruments used in addition to piano are mostly optional, and include recorders or flutes, tuned percussion (glockenspiel, chime bars and xylophone), untuned percussion (tambourine, triangle, drums, cymbals, maracas, claves, guiro, wood-block etc.), and guitar, to supplement or in some cases replace piano. *Cowboy Carol* and *The Holly and the Ivy* also have optional parts for double bass (or bass guitar) and drums, to permit the participation of a pop group (guitar, bass guitar, drums).

Some of the carols are within the capacity of young children, while others include more advanced accompaniments. In these cases, however, instruments may be omitted at will to suit varying resources, and, if desired, accompaniments may be entrusted to piano alone. Most of the carols are lively and rhythmic, which it is hoped will appeal to a wide age group and make teaching and performance enjoyable.

Notes on Performance

Teachers should regard the percussion instruments specified for each carol simply as suggestions. Tuned percussion parts may be played on whatever available instrument is most suitable, and octave transpositions may be freely used; this may be particularly useful where complete sets of chime bars are not available. Two-part chords may be divided between two players on two similar instruments.

Untuned percussion parts are in many cases suitable for instruments other than those specified, and home-made instruments, clapping hands, and stamping feet can often be used. Teachers and pupils should also feel free to vary or simplify the written parts or to invent rhythmic patterns of their own. Many of the untuned percussion parts can be taught by ear.

Most of the guitar parts are given both as chord symbols and in staff notation. None of the parts is difficult, though some are intended for intermediate pupils rather than beginners. In any case, reading from staff notation should be encouraged as early as possible.

Piano parts, though primarily intended for teachers, are in some cases simple enough to be played by pupils.

J.R.

The following three parts are on sale :   Voices/Guitar
Recorders/Flutes
Percussion score

For *Contents* see back cover.

© 1972 **Oxford University Press**
Music Department, Walton Street, Oxford OX2 6DP

CAROLS FOR SCHOOLS

Edited by
John Rutter

1. TYDLIDOM

Words adapted from the Czech
by JOHN RUTTER and others

Czech traditional carol
arranged by
JOHN RUTTER

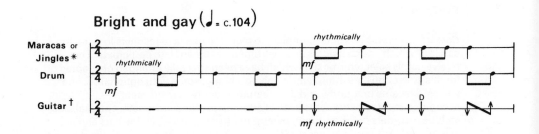

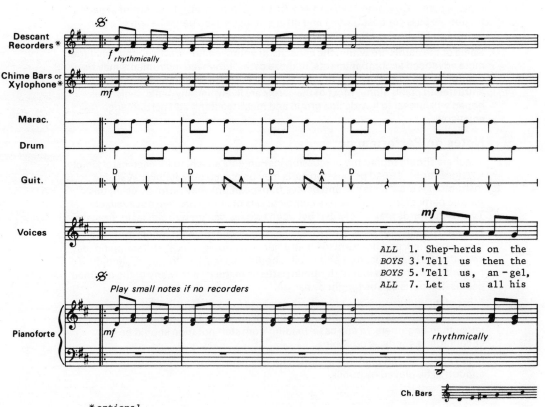

ALL 1. Shep-herds on the
BOYS 3. 'Tell us then the
BOYS 5. 'Tell us, an-gel,
ALL 7. Let us all his

optional

†*Guitar could be dispensed with if piano fills in the chords marked,
in bars where there is no piano part.*

NOTE: *Any other available unpitched percussion may play* ‖: 𝅗𝅥 𝅘𝅥 𝅘𝅥 :‖
or other simple rhythmic patterns during verses 1, 3, 5 and 7.

Melody collected by Vilem Tausky and used by permission

hills at night   Saw a   shin - ing   an - gel   bright.
news you bring,   Tell us   of   this   joy-ful   thing.'
where to find   This the Sa - viour   of   man - kind.'
prais-es   sing,   Wor-ship Christ the   new-born King.

Hy-dom, hy-dom, tyd-li-dom,

hy-dom, hy-dom,   tyd-li-dom.

4

GLOCKENSPIEL

Glock.

mp lightly

Ch.B.

mp lightly

TRIANGLE

Tri.

mp

GIRLS

mp

Voices

2. 'Shep-herds, shep-herds, do not fear;   I   have news to   bring good cheer.'
4. 'On this night is   born a   child,   Hea-ven's King, our   Sa-viour mild.'
6. 'In   a   low-ly   cat-tle stall   You will find the   Lord   of   all.'

*

Pno.

mp lightly

*play small notes if no glockenspiel

†optional

D.S.

Glock.

mf

Ch.B.

mf

Tri.

mf

ALL VOICES

mf

Voices

Hy - dom, hy - dom,   tyd-li - dom,   hy - dom, hy - dom, tyd-li - dom.

D.S.

Pno.

mf

2. LITTLE BULL

Words by A. H. GREEN
from the Spanish

Traditional Latin-American song,
arranged and adapted by
A. H. GREEN

Another version of this carol, arranged by A.H.Green for unison voices, guitar, piano, and optional tambourine, is on sale separately (U 124).

6

see the Vir-gin's Son. He is clothed in white ap - par-el And is bless-ing ev-'ry-

B DESCANT RECORDER or FLUTE *

-one. La la la la la la la la la la la la la la la la la la

* Flute should play an octave higher than written.

la la la la la la la la la la la la la la la la la la la.

PIANO: Tacet from here to **D** if recorder is available.

8

do-ing up so late? And, lit-tle bull, what have you seen On this star-ry Christ-mas E'en?

VERSES 2 and 3 (ALL VOICES)

2. From the tree was born the branch, and From the branch was born the
3. For-ward, for-ward, lit-tle shep-herd, March on brave-ly, ev-'ry-

flower. From the flower was born our La-dy; From our La-dy the sweet Sa-
-one, Thank-ing God with hearts o'er-flow-ing For the gift of his bless-ed

3. STAR CAROL

Words and music by
JOHN RUTTER

1. Sing this night, for a boy is born in Beth-le-hem, Christ our Lord in a
2. An-gels bright, come from hea-ven's high-est glo - ry, Bear the news with its

*Descant recorders may play the specially marked sections of the treble recorder part. They may also double some or all of the voice part.

All instruments other than piano are optional.

The original version of this carol, for mixed voices, optional children's chorus and piano, is on sale (X 233). Scores and parts of an orchestral accompaniment are on hire.

low - ly man - ger lies;   Bring your gifts, come and   wor-ship at his cra - dle,
mes-sage of good cheer: 'Sing, re - joice, for a   King is come to save us,

* *lower voice part is optional throughout.*

Hur-ry   to Beth-le-hem ___ and see the son ___ of   Ma - ry!
Hur-ry   to Beth-le-hem ___ and see the son ___ of   Ma - ry!'

12

* The melody of the refrain is designed to permit the participation of young children.
  Verses may be left to the older children.

† More experienced players may attempt a thumb roll here.

Hur-ry to Beth-le-hem __ and see the son _ of Ma - ry!

(Back to p.10)

SOPRANOS only *p dolce e legato*

3. See, he lies in his

mo-ther's ten-der keep - ing; Je - sus Christ in her lov-ing arms a-sleep.

14

4. Let us all pay our hom-age at the man-ger, Sing his praise on this joy-ful Christ-mas Night; Christ is come, bring-ing pro-mise of sal-va-tion; Hur-ry to Beth-le-hem __ and see the son __ of Ma-ry!

Rec.

(trebles or descants)

Glock.

Ch.B.

Tamb.

Jing.

Tri.

Voices

REFRAIN

See his star   shin-ing bright   In the sky this__ Christ-mas Night!

Pno.

Ped. . . . . . . ✳ sim.

Rec.

(trebles only)

Glock.

Ch.B.

Tamb.

Jing.

Tri.

Voices

Fol - low   me   joy - ful - ly;   Hur-ry   to   Beth - le - hem__

Pno.

Poco largamente

_____ and see the son _____ of Ma - ry, Hur-ry to Beth -le-hem_

_____ and see the son_____ of Ma - ry! _____

* _The upper voice from here to the end is optional._

† _trebles octave higher_

4. I SAW THREE SHIPS

Words traditional

English traditional carol
arranged by
JOHN RUTTER

All instruments other than piano are optional. If guitar is used, piano may be omitted if desired.

After vv. 1 and 3 : straight on for vv. 2 and 4
After v. 5 : to page **20** for v. 6

saw three ships come sail-ing in,
Sa - viour Christ and his la - dy. } *On Christ-mas Day in the morn - ing.*
they sailed in - to Beth-le-hem.

After vv. 1 and 3 : straight on for vv. 2 and 4
After v. 5 : to page **20** for v. 6

BOYS 2. And what was in those ships all three? *On Christ-mas Day, on Christ-mas Day,* And
BOYS 4. Pray, whi-ther sailed those ships all three? Pray,

(Back to p.18)

what was in those ships all three?
whi-ther sailed those ships all three? On Christ-mas Day in the morn - ing.

(Back to p.18)

Play small notes if no high B

ALL 6. And all the bells on earth shall ring, On Christ-mas Day, on Christ-mas Day, And

Play small notes if no ch. bars and glock.

22

* or tambourine roll

molto rall.

ALL 9.Then let us all re-joice a-main! On Christ-mas Day, on Christ-mas Day, Then
let us all re-joice a-main! On Christ-mas Day in the morn - ing.

5. Shepherds Left Their Flocks A-Straying

(Quem pastores)

Words by IMOGEN HOLST
from the original Latin

14th-century German carol
arranged by
JOHN RUTTER

* for voices and/or recorder(s) and/or glockenspiel

For an introduction, it is suggested that one or more recorders
play over the melody line, accompanied by guitar and chime bars only.

Recorders, chime bars and guitar are optional. Piano may be omitted if guitar is used.
If desired, triangle may play ⫶♩ ‡ ‡ | — |♩ ‡ ‡ |♩ ‡ ‡ ⫶ during one or more verses.

Dynamics are left to the teacher's discretion.

Words reprinted by permission of G. & I. Holst Ltd.

for Jane

6. TO BETHLEHEM

Words by
RUTH SAWYER
(tr. from an old Spanish carol)

W. H. PARRY

† *The lower voice part is optional.* *all optional

The poem 'Shall I tell you who will come?' is from The Long Christmas *by Ruth Sawyer (Copyright 1941 by Ruth Sawyer) and is reprinted by arrangement with The Viking Press,Inc.*

This carol is on sale separately, without guitar, (U 132).

tell you   who will come___   To Beth-le-hem___ on Christ-mas morn—

Who will kneel them gent-ly down,   gent-ly down,   gent-ly down Be-

-fore the Lord   new - born?

* *The passage for recorders/flutes marked* ⌐ ¬ *may be substituted for that similarly marked in the final refrain on pages* **28** *and* **29** *.*

Rec.
Mar.
Tri.
Guit.
Voices
Pno.

A   A susp.2   A   Bm7   D(E bass)   E9   E7

Rec.
Mar.
Tamb.
Tri.
Guit.
Voices
Pno.

mp smoothly

A   Dm7   G7   Cmaj.7   Fmaj.7   Dm

mp
p (2nd time mf)

smoothly

p 1. One small fish   from the   riv - er____   With scales of red, red
mf 2. And one   ox   from the   pas - ture,___   One black bull from the

p (2nd time mf)

dim. e poco rit.

Rec.
Guit.
Voices
Pno.

Em   Bm   F♯m   G   Bm   F♯m

gold,   One   wild bee   from the   hea - ther,   One   grey___ lamb from the
herd,   One   year-ling   from the   far hills,   One   white,__ white____

dim. e poco rit.

Slower

And ma-ny chil-dren,____ God give them grace,____ Bring-ing tall

tenuto__a tempo

can-dles to light Ma-ry's face.____ Shall I tell you who will

tenuto__a tempo

come____ To Beth-le-hem__ On Christ-mas morn— Who will kneel them

* see footnote on page 25

7. SILENT NIGHT
(Stille Nacht)

Words from the German of
JOSEF MOHR

FRANZ GRUBER
arranged by
JOHN RUTTER

Recorders, glockenspiel and chime bars are optional. Piano part should be used only in the absence of guitar.

* 2nd voice part is optional, but if it is omitted, recorders or piano should double both voice parts.

* *small notes for 2nd recorder*

for S.P.G.S.

8. THE HOLLY AND THE IVY

Words traditional

JOHN GARDNER
Op. 58 No. 2
adapted by
JOHN RUTTER

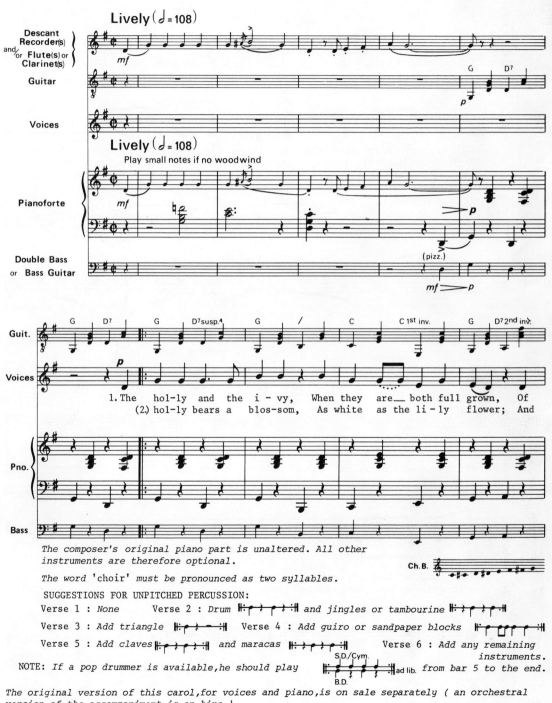

The composer's original piano part is unaltered. All other instruments are therefore optional.

The word 'choir' must be pronounced as two syllables.

SUGGESTIONS FOR UNPITCHED PERCUSSION:

Verse 1 : *None*   Verse 2 : *Drum* and *jingles or tambourine*

Verse 3 : *Add triangle*   Verse 4 : *Add guiro or sandpaper blocks*

Verse 5 : *Add claves* and *maracas*   Verse 6 : *Add any remaining instruments.*

NOTE: *If a pop drummer is available, he should play* ad lib. *from bar 5 to the end.*

The original version of this carol, for voices and piano, is on sale separately (an orchestral version of the accompaniment is on hire).

34

hol-ly bears a ber-ry, As red as a-ny blood, And Ma-ry bore sweet
hol-ly bears a prick-le, As sharp as a-ny thorn, And Ma-ry bore sweet

* *Optional small notes, originally for clarinet, may be taken by flute or expert recorder player, or else played on the piano by a third hand.*

Je-sus Christ To do poor sin-ners__ good: The ris-ing of the
Je-sus Christ On Christ-mas Day in the morn:

Je-sus Christ To do poor sin-ners__ good: The ris-ing
Je-sus Christ On Christ-mas Day in the morn:

sun, And the run-ning of the deer, The play-ing of the

of the sun, ___ And the run-ning of the deer, ___ The play-ing

merry organ, Sweet singing in the choir. ___ 4. The

of the merry organ, Sweet singing in the choir. ___ 4. The

RECORDERS
Verse 6 only

GUITAR

5. The holly bears a bark, As bitter as any gall, And
(6.) holly and the ivy, When they___ are both full grown, Of

36

to David

9. REJOICE AND BE MERRY

Words from an old
Church Gallery book (Dorset)

J. ALBAN HINTON

Recorders, chime bars, and glockenspiel/handbells are optional.

The original version of this carol, which includes a fuller version of the piano accompaniment to verse 4, is on sale separately.

The accompaniment to this carol is also scored for strings and piano, with optional parts for flute, clarinet, horn, descant recorders, and handbells or chime bars. Scores and parts are on hire.

In the present version the percussion parts have been slightly altered.

Words from the Oxford Book of Carols by permission.

39

40

*Glockenspiel or handbells continue to bar 71 if desired.

4. And when they were come, they their trea-sures un-fold, And
un-to him off-ered myrrh, in-cense, and gold. So bless-ed for ev-er be Je-sus our
King Who brought us sal - va-tion-his prai - - ses we'll sing!

10. ZITHER CAROL

Words by
MALCOLM SARGENT

Czech folk tune
arranged by
MALCOLM SARGENT

*'zing'- to be pronounced 'tzing'. All slurred notes to be sung legato and with glissando

The original version of this carol, for voices and piano, is on sale separately (U 84).

† Sargent's original piano part is unaltered. All other instruments are therefore optional, but if guitar is used, piano is best omitted. Percussion instruments should be varied and omitted during different verses, at teacher's discretion.

2. **p** On that day – far away – Jesus lay,
      Angels were watching round his head.
      Holy Child – Mother mild – undefiled,
   cresc. We sing thy praise.

        f   *'Hallelujah' etc.*

       Our hearts we raise.

3. **mf** Shepherds came – at the fame – of thy name,
      Angels their guide to Bethlehem.
      In that place – saw thy face – filled with grace,
      Stood at thy door.

        f   *'Hallelujah' etc.*

       Love evermore.

4. **mf** Wise men too – haste to do – homage new,
      Gold, myrrh and frankincense they bring.
      As 'twas said – starlight led – to thy bed,
   p Bending their knee.

        f   *'Hallelujah' etc.*

       Worshipping thee.

5. **pp** Oh, that we – all might be – good as he,
      Spotless, with God in Unity.
   cresc. Saviour dear – ever near – with us here
      Since life began.

        f   *'Hallelujah' etc.*

       Godhead made man.

6.   **f** Cherubim – Seraphim – worship him,
      Sun, moon and stars proclaim his power.
      Everyday – on our way – we shall say
     ff Hallelujah.

        ff *'Hallelujah' etc.*

       Hallelujah.

11. SHEPHERD'S PIPE CAROL

Words and music by
JOHN RUTTER

BOYS 1. Go-ing through the hills on a night all star - ry On the way to Beth-le-hem,
BOYS 2. Tell me, shep-herd boy pip-ing tunes so mer-ri-ly On the way to Beth-le-hem,

† *all optional*

⊕ *This part may also be played on the piano by a third hand, an octave higher than written. If played on the flute alone, it should also be played an octave higher. For a solo piano version of the accompaniment, see the original mixed voice (X 167) or unison (U 133) arrangements.*

* *The boys-girls division is optional and may be reversed when unbroken boys' voices are used, in order that the part for the shepherd boy may be sung by boys.*

* lower voices take small notes.

48

cra-dled there at Beth-le-hem.'

GIRLS 3. 'None may hear my pipes on these hills so lone-ly On the way to Beth-le-hem,

But a King will hear me play sweet lul-la-bies When I get to Beth-le-hem.'

50

BOYS 4. 'Where is this new King, shep-herd boy pip-ing mer-ri-ly, Is he there at Beth - le-hem?'

GIRLS 'I will find him soon by the star shin-ing bright-ly

53

† for unbroken voices only

An - gels in__ the sky brought this mes - sage nigh:

An - gels__ brought this mes - sage:

'Dance and sing for joy that Christ the in-fant King is

'Dance and sing for joy that Christ the in-fant King is

56

12. COWBOY CAROL

Words and melody by
CECIL BROADHURST

Arranged by
MALCOLM SARGENT

† or a pair of wood blocks, coconut shells or clicked tongues
(at teacher's discretion).

Ch.B.

* Sargent's original piano part is unaltered. All other instruments are therefore optional,
but if guitar is used, piano is best omitted. If a pop drummer is available, he may play
ad lib. except during the bars of rallentando.

This carol is on sale separately, with piano accompaniment only (U88).

Words and melody from The Cowboy Christmas by permission of The Oxford Group

58

* Play small notes if chime bars are used.

59

62

64